DEVOTIONS
FOR
RENEWAL
& JOY

ROMANS & PHILIPPIANS

DEVOTIONS
FOR
RENEWAL
& JOY

ROMANS & PHILIPPIANS

Warren W. Wiersbe

HONOR  BOOKS

Inspiration and Motivation for the Seasons of Life

COOK COMMUNICATIONS MINISTRIES
Colorado Springs, Colorado • Paris, Ontario
KINGSWAY COMMUNICATIONS LTD
Eastbourne, England

Honor® is an imprint of
Cook Communications Ministries, Colorado Springs, CO 80918
Cook Communications, Paris, Ontario
Kingsway Communications, Eastbourne, England

DEVOTIONS FOR RENEWAL AND JOY
© 2005 by Warren Wiersbe

Cover Design: Jackson Design CO, LLC/Greg Jackson

First Printing, 2005
Printed in the United States of America

Printing/Year
1 2 3 4 5 6 7 8 9 10 / 10 09 08 07 06 05

This book was originally published as two paperback editions in 1994 and 1995, compiled by Stan Campbell. Each devotional reading is adapted from Warren Wiersbe's "Be" series.

ISBN 1-56292-698-5

Renewal

Thirty Daily Readings from the Book of Romans

Y ou've probably noticed during political campaigns that many of the candidates promise to do "new things" to solve the old problems. Whether it's a "new frontier" or a "new deal" or a "new vision," the promise is the same: It's time for renewal. It's time for a change!

When Paul wrote to the Christians in Rome, one of his themes was *making a new beginning*. He explained how the gospel of Jesus Christ is the answer to the "old problems" everybody confronts—problems like sin, guilt, defeat, and broken relationships. The heart of every problem is the problem of the heart, and only through Jesus Christ can we have new hearts so that we can make new beginnings in life.

Renewal begins with a new relationship with God, which Paul calls *justification,* a basic biblical doctrine that every child of God must understand. Spiritual renewal that begins with justification continues with *sanctification,* a new power to overcome sin and a new motive for living. Paul tells us how the new life in Christ enables us to be good friends, good citizens, and good servants of God in the midst of a wicked world.

As Paul reasons about God's marvelous plan of salvation and explains how it works, you'll discover how practical this "renewed life" really is, and how "justified" people can experience renewal—"newness of life"—in their daily walk with the Lord.

It's time for a change! It's time for renewal! And the epistle to the Romans points the way.

"We know that suffering produces perseverence;
perseverence, character; and character, hope."

Day 1

The Right Stuff

Read Romans 1:1–7

"You also are among those who are called to belong to Jesus Christ."
ROMANS 1:6

When we study the book of Romans, we walk into a courtroom. First, Paul called Jews and Gentiles to the stand and found both guilty before God. Then he explained God's marvelous way of salvation—justification by faith. At this point, he answered his accusers and defended God's salvation. "This plan of salvation will encourage people to sin!" they cried. "It is against the very law of God!" But Paul refuted them, and in so doing explained how Christians could experience victory, liberty, and security.

There were Jewish believers in the Roman assemblies and they would naturally ask, "What about Israel? How does God's righteousness relate to them in this new age of the church?" In chapters 9–11 Paul gave a complete history of Israel, past, present, and future.

Then he concluded with the practical outworking of God's righteousness in the life of believers. When we sum it all up, in the book of Romans Paul is saying to us—"Be *right!* Be right with God, with yourself, and with others!" The righteousness of God received by faith makes it possible for us to live right lives. The Romans needed this message then, and we need it today: *Be right!*

Applying God's Truth:

1. What is one situation you're facing where you need to experience more victory? Liberty? Security?

2. How has God's righteousness been evident in your past? Your present? How do you expect Him to work in your future?

3. What are your goals as you begin to read through the book of Romans?

Day 2

When in Rome . . .

Read Romans 1:8–15

"I am obligated both to Greeks and non-Greeks, both to the wise and the foolish.
That is why I am so eager to preach the gospel also to you who are at Rome."
ROMANS 1:14–15

Paul's special commission was to take the gospel to the Gentiles, and this is why he was planning to go to Rome, the very capital of the empire. He was a preacher of the gospel, and the gospel was for all nations.

Rome was a proud city, and the gospel came from Jerusalem, the capital city of one of the little nations that Rome had conquered. The Christians in that day were not among the elite of society; they were common people and even slaves. Rome had known many great philosophers and philosophies; why pay any attention to a fable about a Jew who arose from the dead? Christians looked upon each other as brothers and sisters, all one in Christ, which went against the grain of Roman pride and dignity. To think of a little Jewish tentmaker going to Rome to preach such a message is almost humorous.

Paul arrived in Rome a prisoner as well as a preacher. In Jerusalem he was arrested in the temple, falsely accused by the Jewish authorities, and eventually sent to Rome as the emperor's prisoner to be tried before Caesar. When Paul wrote this letter, he had no idea that he would go through imprisonment and even shipwreck before arriving in Rome! At the close of the letter (see 15:30–33), he asked the believers in Rome to pray for him as he contemplated this trip, and it is a good thing that they did pray!

Applying God's Truth:

1. Paul directly confronted the pride of Rome. What are some of the obstacles *you* face as you try to present the gospel to others?

2. If you knew that presenting the truth of Jesus to others would involve shipwreck, imprisonment, and other similar hardships, would you be at all reluctant to share the gospel? Why or why not?

3. Do you have the assurance of knowing that other people are praying for you? If not, what can you do to arrange some prayer support?

Day 3

Luther, Wesley ... and You?

Read Romans 1:16–17

"In the gospel a righteousness from God is revealed, a righteousness that is by faith from first to last, just as it is written: 'The righteous will live by faith.'"

ROMANS 1:17

On May 24, 1738, a discouraged missionary went "very unwillingly" to a religious meeting in London. There a miracle took place. "About a quarter before nine," he wrote in his journal, "I felt my heart strangely warmed. I felt I did trust in Christ, Christ alone, for salvation; and an assurance was given me that He had taken away my sins, even mine, and saved me from the law of sin and death."

That missionary was John Wesley. The message he heard that evening was the preface to Martin Luther's commentary on Romans. Paul's epistle to the Romans is still transforming people's lives, just the way it transformed Martin Luther and John Wesley. The one Scripture above all others that brought Luther out of mere religion into the joy of salvation by grace, through faith, was verse 17: "The righteous will live by faith." The Protestant Reformation and the Wesleyan revival were both the fruit of this wonderful letter.

Imagine! You and I can read and study the same inspired letter that brought life and power to Luther and Wesley! And the same Holy Spirit who taught them can teach us! You and I can experience revival in our hearts, homes, and churches if the message of this letter grips us as it gripped people of faith in centuries past.

Applying God's Truth:

1. What do you think would need to happen before you could experience revival in your church? In your home? In your personal life?

2. What is the number one transformation you desire for your life?

3. Why do you think the message of "living by faith" made such a difference for Luther and Wesley?

Day 4

Accept No Substitutes

Read Romans 1:18–32

> *"Although they knew God, they neither glorified him as God*
> *nor gave thanks to him, but their thinking became futile*
> *and their foolish hearts were darkened."*
>
> ROMANS 1:21

Man knew God; this is clear. But man did not want to know God or honor Him as God. Instead of being thankful for all that God had given him, man refused to thank God or give Him the glory He deserves. Man was willing to use God's gifts, but he was not willing to worship and praise God for His gifts. The result was an empty mind and a darkened heart. Man the worshiper became man the philosopher, but his empty wisdom only revealed his foolishness.

Having held down God's truth and refusing to acknowledge God's glory, man was left without a god; and man is so constituted that he must worship something. If he will not worship the true God, he will worship a false god, *even if he has to manufacture it himself!* This fact about man accounts for his propensity to idolatry. Man exchanged the glory of the true God for substitute gods that he himself made. He exchanged glory for shame, incorruption for corruption, truth for lies.

Applying God's Truth:

1. Why do you think some people are so resistant to honoring God?

2. What are some false gods that people today turn to?

3. Do you personally know people who reject God and turn to substitutes? Can you do anything to influence and/or help these people?

Day 5

Consistent Actions

Read Romans 2:1–3:20

*"To those who by persistence in doing good seek glory, honor and immortality,
he will give eternal life. But for those who are self-seeking and who reject
the truth and follow evil, there will be wrath and anger."*

ROMANS 2:7–8

God had given Israel great material and spiritual riches: a wonderful land, a righteous law, a temple and priesthood, God's providential care, and many more blessings. God had patiently endured Israel's many sins and rebellions, and He even sent them His Son to be their Messiah. Even after Israel crucified Christ, God gave the nation nearly forty more years of grace and withheld His judgment. It is not the *judgment* of God that leads people to repentance, but the *goodness* of God; but Israel did not repent.

In verses 6–11 of chapter 2, Paul was not teaching salvation by character or good deeds. He was explaining another basic principle of God's judgment: God judges according to deeds, just as He judges according to truth. Paul was dealing here with the consistent actions of people's lives, the total impact of their character and conduct.

True saving faith results in obedience and godly living, even though there may be occasional falls. When God measured the deeds of the Jews, He found them to be as wicked as those of the Gentiles.

Applying God's Truth:

1. What are some obvious blessings of God that people—even many Christians—tend to overlook too often?

2. How does the goodness of God lead people to repentance?

3. Unsaved people can certainly do good things. Do you think they can *consistently* have good character and conduct? Explain.

Day 6

Cost versus Value

Read Romans 3:21–31

"All have sinned and fall short of the glory of God, and are justified freely by his grace through the redemption that came by Christ Jesus."

ROMANS 3:23–24

Salvation is free, but it is not cheap. Jesus had to die on the cross in order to satisfy the law and justify lost sinners. The best illustration of this truth is the Jewish Day of Atonement described in Leviticus 16. Two goats were presented at the altar, and one of them was chosen for a sacrifice. The priest then put his hands on the head of the other goat and confessed the sins of the people. Then the goat was taken out into the wilderness and set free to symbolize the carrying away of sins.

Dr. G. Campbell Morgan was trying to explain "free salvation" to a coal miner, but the man was unable to understand it. "I have to pay for it," he kept arguing. With a flash of divine insight, Dr. Morgan asked, "How did you get down into the mine this morning?" "Why, it was easy," the man replied. "I just got on the elevator and went down."

Then Morgan asked, "Wasn't that too easy? Didn't it cost you something?"

The man laughed. "No, it didn't cost me anything, but it must have cost the company plenty to install that elevator." Then the man saw the truth: "It doesn't cost *me* anything to be saved, but it cost *God* the life of His Son."

Applying God's Truth:

1. How do you think the phrase "You get what you pay for" applies to salvation?

2. Does the fact that your salvation is free mean that you're under no obligation to God? Explain.

3. Can you think of an analogy for a specific unsaved friend that would parallel the elevator anecdote used with the coal miner?

Day 7

Some Things Never Change

Read Romans 4:1–15

> *"What does the Scripture say? 'Abraham believed God,
> and it was credited to him as righteousness.'"*
>
> ROMANS 4:3

Dr. Harry Ironside, for eighteen years pastor of Moody Church in Chicago, told of visiting a Sunday school class while on vacation. The teacher asked, "How were people saved in Old Testament times?"

After a pause, one man replied, "By keeping the law."

"That's right," said the teacher.

But Dr. Ironside interrupted: "My Bible says that by the deeds of the law shall no flesh be justified" (see Rom. 3:20 KJV).

The teacher was a bit embarrassed, so he said, "Well, does somebody else have an idea?"

Another student replied, "They were saved by bringing sacrifices to God."

"Yes, that's right!" the teacher said, and tried to go on with the lesson.

But Dr. Ironside interrupted, "My Bible says that the blood of bulls and goats cannot take away sin" (see Heb. 10:4).

By this time the unprepared teacher was sure the visitor knew more about the Bible than he did, so he said, "Well, *you* tell us how people were saved in the Old Testament!"

And Dr. Ironside explained that they were saved by faith—the same way people are saved today! (see Eph. 2:8–9).

The Bible says that Abraham "believed God, and it was credited to him as righteousness" (Rom. 4:3) He is the father of all who believe on Jesus Christ and are justified by faith (see v. 11). Although Gentiles can never be natural descendants of Abraham, they can be his *spiritual* descendants—by faith.

Applying God's Truth:

1. Prior to this reading, how would you have responded to the question: "How were people saved in Old Testament times?"

2. Since faith was behind the ceremonies of the Old Testament, what should faith inspire *us* to do today?

3. What do you think is entailed in being a "spiritual descendant" of Abraham (privileges, responsibilities, etc.)?

Day 8

A Legal Matter

Read Romans 4:16–25

> *"[Jesus our Lord] was delivered over to death for our sins
> and was raised to life for our justification."*
> ROMANS 4:25

Justification is the act of God whereby He declares believing sinners righteous in Christ on the basis of the finished work of Christ on the cross. Each part of this definition is important, so we must consider it carefully.

To begin with, justification is an act, not a process. There are no degrees of justification; each of us believers has the same right standing before God. Also, justification is something done by *God*, not by us. As sinners, we cannot justify ourselves before God. Most important, justification does not mean that God makes us righteous, but that He declares us righteous. Justification is a legal matter. God puts the righteousness of Christ on our record in the place of our own sinfulness. And nobody can change this record.

We must not confuse justification and sanctification. Sanctification is the process whereby God makes us believers more and more like Christ. Sanctification may change from day to day. Justification never changes. When we trust Christ, God declares us righteous, and that declaration will never be repealed. God looks upon us and deals with us as though we had never sinned at all!

Applying God's Truth:

1. Since justification is an *act* of *God*, what is *your* responsibility?

2. Can you give a personal example to explain the difference between justification and sanctification?

3. Do you feel you have a good understanding of justification and sanctification? If not, what resources and people can you consult?

Day 9

The Hope Sequence

Read Romans 5:1–11

> *"We know that suffering produces perseverance;*
> *perseverance, character; and character, hope."*
>
> ROMANS 5:3–4

Justification is no escape from the trials of life. But as believers, our trials work *for* us and not *against* us. Suffering builds Christian character. The sequence is: suffering—perseverance—character—hope. Our English word "tribulation" comes from a Latin word *tribulum*. In Paul's day, a *tribulum* was a heavy piece of timber with spikes in it, used for threshing the grain. The *tribulum* was drawn over the grain, and it separated the wheat from the chaff. As we go through tribulations, and depend on God's grace, the trials only purify us and help to get rid of the chaff.

For many months I visited a young man in a hospital who had almost burned to death. I do not know how many operations and skin grafts he had during those months or how many specialists visited him. But the thing that sustained him during those difficult months was not the explanations of the doctors, but the promises they gave him that he would recover. That was his hope. And the thing that sustained his hope was the love of his family and many friends as they stood by him. The love of God was channeled through them to him. He did recover and today gives glory to God.

Applying God's Truth:

1. Do you think it's possible to have perseverance, character, and hope *without* sufferings? Explain.

2. Can you think of a recent personal trial that helped make you a better, stronger person?

3. How can personal trials result in your giving glory to God?

Day 10

We Need a Good Reign

Read Romans 5:12–21

"But where sin increased, grace increased all the more, so that, just as sin reigned in death, so also grace might reign through righteousness to bring eternal life through Jesus Christ our Lord."

ROMANS 5:20–21

Grace was not an addition to God's plan; grace was a part of God's plan from the very beginning. God dealt with Adam and Eve in grace; He dealt with the patriarchs in grace; and He dealt with the nation of Israel in grace. He gave the law through Moses, not to replace His grace, but to reveal man's need for grace. Law was temporary, but grace is eternal.

But as the law made man's sins increase, God's grace increased even more. God's grace was more than adequate to deal with man's sins. Even though sin and death still reign in this world, God's grace is also reigning through the righteousness of Christ.

An Old Testament story helps us understand the conflict between these two "reigns" in the world today. God rejected Saul as the king of Israel, and anointed David. Those who trusted David eventually shared his kingdom of peace and joy. Those who trusted Saul ended in shame and defeat (see 1 Sam. chaps. 9–31).

Like David, Jesus Christ is God's anointed King. Like Saul, Satan is still free to work in this world and seek to win people's allegiance. Sin and death are reigning in the "old creation" over which Adam was the head, but grace and righteousness are reigning in "the new creation" over which Christ is the Head. And as we yield to Him, we "reign in life" (Rom. 5:17).

Applying God's Truth:

1. What is your definition of God's "grace"? What is a personal example?

2. Without God's grace, how do you think the religion of Christianity would be different?

3. To what extent do *people* determine which of the two "reigns" is more in control?

Day 11

The Living Dead

Read Romans 6:1–4

> *"We were therefore buried with him through baptism into death in order that, just as Christ was raised from the dead through the glory of the Father, we too may live a new life."*
>
> ROMANS 6:4

Historians agree that the mode of baptism in the early church was immersion. Believers were "buried" in the water and brought up again as a picture of death, burial, and resurrection. Baptism by immersion (which is the illustration Paul is using in Romans 6) pictures believers' identification with Christ in His death, burial, and resurrection. It is an outward symbol of an inward experience. Paul is not saying that their immersion in water put them "into Jesus Christ," for that was accomplished by the Spirit when they believed. Their immersion was a picture of what the Holy Spirit did: He identified them with Christ in His death, burial, and resurrection.

This means that believers have a new relationship to sin. They are "dead to sin" (v. 11). If an alcoholic dies, he can no longer be tempted by alcohol because his body is dead to all physical senses. He cannot see the alcohol, smell it, taste it, or desire it. In Jesus Christ we have died to sin so that we no longer want to "continue in sin" (v. 1 KJV). But we are not only dead to sin; we are also alive in Christ. We have been raised from the dead and now walk in the power of His resurrection. We walk in "newness of life" (v. 4 KJV) because we share His life. Like Paul, each of us can now say, "I have been crucified with Christ and I no longer live, but Christ lives in me" (Gal. 2:20).

Applying God's Truth:

1. In what ways have you demonstrated that you have "died to sin"?

2. Which sins do you find most difficult to remain "dead" to?

3. What steps do you take to "stay dead" when tempted by old and alluring sins?

Day 12

Don't Be a "Betweener"

Read Romans 6:5–23

"Anyone who has died has been freed from sin."
ROMANS 6:7

Too many Christians are "betweeners": They live between Egypt and Canaan, saved but never satisfied; or they live between Good Friday and Easter, believing in the Cross but not entering into the power and glory of the Resurrection.

A tremendous fact is introduced in verse 6 of this section of Romans. The "old man" (the ego, the self) was crucified with Christ so that the body need not be controlled by sin. The phrase "done away with" in verse 6 does not mean annihilated; it means "rendered inactive, made of no effect."

Sin wants to be our master. It finds a foothold in the old nature, and through the old nature seeks to control the members of the body. But in Jesus Christ, we died to sin, and the old nature was crucified so that the old life is rendered inoperative. Paul was not describing an experience; he was stating a fact. The practical experience was to come later. It is a fact of history that believers have died with Him, and "anyone who has died has been freed from sin" (v. 7). Not "free *to* sin" as Paul's accusers falsely stated, but "freed *from* sin."

Applying God's Truth:

1. How do you feel about being "united with [Jesus] … in his death"? (See v. 5.) Why?

2. Using a percentage, to what extent do you feel you've "entered into the power and glory of the Resurrection"?

3. What things can you do to experience more fully the life and freedom Jesus has made possible for you?

Day 13

Two Extremes

Read Romans 7:1–6

"By dying to what once bound us, we have been released from the law so that we serve in the new way of the Spirit, and not in the old way of the written code."

ROMANS 7:6

Something in human nature makes people want to go to extremes, a weakness from which Christians are not wholly immune. "Since we are saved by grace," some argue, "we are free to live as we please," which is the law of *license*.

"But we cannot ignore God's law," others argue. "We are saved by grace, to be sure; but we must live under law if we are to please God." This is the extreme expression of *legalism*.

What really is "legalism"? It is the belief that human beings can become holy and please God by obeying laws. It is measuring spirituality by a list of dos and don'ts. The weakness of legalism is that it sees *sins* (plural, acts of the flesh) but not *sin* (singular, the root of the trouble).

In my pastoral experience, I have counseled many people who have suffered severe emotional and spiritual damage because they have tried to live holy lives on the basis of a high moral standard. I have seen the consequences of these attempts: Either such people become pretenders, or they suffer a complete collapse and abandon all desires for godly living. I have seen, too, that many legalists are extremely hard on other people—critical, unloving, unforgiving. Paul wanted to spare his readers this difficult and dangerous experience.

Applying God's Truth:

1. Do you tend to lean more toward the extreme of license or the extreme of legalism? In what ways?

2. What do you feel are the major problems that result from legalism?

3. How would you suggest that people could remain absolutely obedient and faithful to God without falling into the snare of legalism?

Day 14

The Rebel Within

Read Romans 7:7–13

> *"But sin, seizing the opportunity afforded by the commandment, produced in me every kind of covetous desire. For apart from law, sin is dead."*
>
> ROMANS 7:8

Something in human nature wants to rebel whenever a law is given. I was standing in Lincoln Park in Chicago, looking at the newly painted benches; and I noticed a sign on each bench: "Do Not Touch." As I watched, I saw numbers of people deliberately reach out and touch the wet paint! Why? Because the sign told them not to! If a child is told not to go near the water, that is the very thing the little darling will do! Why? Because "the sinful mind is hostile to God. It does not submit to God's law, nor can it do so" (Rom. 8:7).

Believers who try to live by rules and regulations discover that their legalistic system only arouses more desires and creates more sin problems. The churches in Galatia were very legalistic, and they experienced all kinds of trouble. "If you keep on biting and devouring each other," Paul warned them, "watch out or you will be destroyed by each other" (Gal. 5:15). Their legalism did not make them more spiritual; it made them more sinful! Why? Because the law arouses sin in human nature.

Applying God's Truth:

1. What rules and regulations do you find most frustrating? Why?

2. What are some forbidden things that tend to arouse your curiosity or attract your interest?

3. If rules and regulations are a source of problems, should they be done away with? If not, what other options are there?

Day 15

Human Error

Read Romans 7:14–25

*"I do not understand what I do. For what I want to
do I do not do, but what I hate I do."*

ROMANS 7:15

The law cannot give life—it can only show sinners that they are
guilty and condemned. This truth explains why legalistic
Christians and churches do not grow and bear spiritual fruit. They are
living by law, and the law always kills (see 2 Cor. 3:6). Few things are
deader than a legalistic church that is proud of its "high standards"
and tries to live up to them in its own energy. Often the members of
such a church start to judge and condemn one another, and the sad
result is a church fight and then a church split that leaves members—
or former members—angry and bitter.

As new Christians grow, they often come into contact with various
philosophies of the Christian life. They may read books, attend semi-
nars, listen to tapes, and get a great deal of information. If they are not
careful, they will start following human leaders and accepting their
teachings as law. This practice is a very subtle form of legalism, and it
kills spiritual growth. No human teacher can take the place of Christ;
no book can take the place of the Bible.

Human beings can give us information, but only the Spirit can
give us illumination and help us understand spiritual truths. The
Spirit enlightens us and enables us; no human leader can do that.

Applying God's Truth:

1. What are some mistakes you've made in the past when trying to eliminate a difficult problem? Did you possibly put too much trust in a human resource rather than a godly one?

2. Who are some celebrities who promise answers to various personal problems? Why do you think people "buy into" so much blatant self-promotion and sales tactics?

3. How can you benefit from the wisdom of other people without putting too much value on their advice?

Day 16

Levels of Life

Read Romans 8:1–17

"Those who are led by the Spirit of God are sons of God."
ROMANS 8:14

To be unsaved and not have the Spirit is the lowest level of life. But people need not stay on that level. By faith in Christ they can move to the second level. The evidence of conversion is the presence of the Holy Spirit within, witnessing that believers are children of God (see v. 16). Their body becomes the very temple of the Holy Spirit (see 1 Cor. 6:19).

What a difference it makes in our body when the Holy Spirit lives within us. We experience new life, and even our physical faculties take on a new dimension of experience. When evangelist D. L. Moody described his conversion experience, he said: "I was in a new world. The next morning the sun shone brighter and the birds sang sweeter … the old elms waved their branches for joy, and all nature was at peace." Life in Christ is abundant life (see John 10:10).

But there is a third level of experience for which the other two are preparation. It is not enough for us to have the Spirit; the Spirit must have us! (See Rom. 8:12–17.) Only then can He share with us the abundant, victorious life that can be ours in Christ. Because He is "the Spirit of life" (v. 6), He can empower us to obey Christ, and He can enable us to be more like Christ.

Applying God's Truth:

1. What friends can you think of in each of the three levels of life: (1) those who do not have God's Spirit; (2) those who do have the Spirit; and (3) those under the control of the Spirit?

2. How has the Holy Spirit changed your perspective on life?

3. Can you think of ways to allow God's Holy Spirit to have more control over you?

Day 17

No Condemnation

Read Romans 8:18–39

> *"We know that in all things God works for the good of those who love him, who have been called according to his purpose."*
>
> ROMANS 8:28

As believers we never need faint in times of suffering and trial because we know that God is at work in the world, and that He has a perfect plan for us (see vv. 28–29). God has two purposes in that plan: our good and His glory. Ultimately, He will make us like Jesus Christ! (See v. 29.) Best of all, God's plan is going to succeed!

Why should we Christians ever be discouraged and frustrated when we already share the glory of God? Our suffering today only guarantees that much more glory when Jesus Christ returns!

There is no condemnation because we share the righteousness of God, and the law cannot condemn us. There is no obligation because we have the Spirit of God who enables us to overcome the flesh and live for God. There is no frustration because we share the glory of God, the blessed hope of Christ's return. There is no separation because we experience the love of Christ (see v. 35). We do not need to fear the past, the present, or the future because we are secure in "the love of God that is in Jesus Christ our Lord" (v. 39).

Applying God's Truth:

1. Looking back over your life, can you see how some of your trying situations have resulted in good?

2. What is one thing you are suffering with right now for which you can see no possible way for God ever to use for good? Do you have the faith to trust Him to do so?

3. Can you truthfully say that you feel no condemnation from God? No obligation? No frustration? No separation? Which of these areas do you feel needs the most attention?

Day 18

An Emphasis on Israel

Read Romans 9:1–13

> *"I could wish that I myself were cursed and cut off from Christ for the sake of my brothers, those of my own race, the people of Israel."*
>
> ROMANS 9:3–4

It seems strange that Paul would interrupt his discussion of salvation and devote a long section of three chapters to the nation of Israel. Why didn't he move from the doctrinal teaching of chapter 8 to the practical duties given in chapters 12 through 15?

To begin with, Paul was considered a traitor to the Jewish nation. He ministered to Gentiles, and he taught freedom from the law of Moses. He had preached in many synagogues and caused trouble, and no doubt many of the Jewish believers in Rome had heard of his questionable reputation. In these chapters, Paul showed his love for Israel and his desire for their welfare. This was the personal reason for this discussion.

But there was a doctrinal reason. Paul had argued in Romans 8 that believers are secure in Jesus Christ and that God's election would stand. But someone might have asked, "What about the Jews? They were chosen by God, and yet now you tell us they are set aside, and God is building His church. Has God failed to keep His promises to Israel?" In other words, the very character of God was at stake.

So the emphasis in chapter 9 is on Israel's past election, in chapter 10 on Israel's present rejection, and in chapter 11 on Israel's future restoration. Israel is the only nation in the world with a complete history—past, present, and future.

Applying God's Truth:

1. Of what you know about Israel's history, what would you say were its most glorious periods? Its lowest points?

2. If you had been a devout Jew during the first century, how do you think you would have felt about Paul? Why?

3. What do you think God has in mind for Israel's future?

Day 19

Justice, Mercy, and Sovereignty

Read Romans 9:14–21

> *"Is God unjust? Not at all! For he says to Moses, 'I will have mercy on whom I have mercy, and I will have compassion on whom I have compassion.'"*
>
> ROMANS 9:14–15

Moses was a Jew, Pharaoh was a Gentile, yet both were sinners. In fact, both were murderers! Both saw God's wonders. Yet Moses was saved and Pharaoh was lost. God raised up Pharaoh to a position of authority that He might reveal His glory and power (see v. 17); and He had mercy on Moses that He might use him to deliver the people of Israel. Pharaoh was a ruler, and Moses was a slave, yet it was Moses who experienced the mercy and compassion of God—because God willed it that way. God is sovereign in His work and acts according to His own will and purposes. So it was not a matter of righteousness but of the sovereign will of God.

God is holy and must punish sin, but God is loving and desires to save sinners. If everybody were saved, it would deny His holiness, but if everybody were lost, it would deny His love. The solution to the problem is God's sovereign election.

A seminary professor once said to me, "Try to explain election, and you may lose your mind; but explain it away, and you will lose your soul."

God chose Israel and condemned Egypt, because it was His sovereign purpose. Nobody can condemn God for the way He extends His mercy, because God is righteous in His judgments (see Ps. 19:9 KJV).

Applying God's Truth:

1. As you read this section of Romans, do any questions come to mind? If so, with whom can you discuss your questions?

2. When God shows mercy to some people, does that mean He's being unfair to others? Why?

3. When you can't fully understand God's working, what do you do to maintain your faith?

Day 20

Grace Righteousness versus Law Righteousness

❧

Read Romans 9:22–33

> "The Gentiles, who did not pursue righteousness, have obtained it,
> a righteousness that is by faith; but Israel, who pursued a
> law of righteousness, has not attained it."
>
> ROMANS 9:30–31

Paul wrote of divine sovereignty and then human responsibility. Note that Paul did not say "elect" and "nonelect," but rather emphasized faith. Here is a paradox: The Jews sought for righteousness but did not find it, while the Gentiles, who were not searching for it, found it! The reason? Israel tried to be saved by works and not by faith. They rejected "grace righteousness" and tried to please God with "law righteousness." The Jews thought that the Gentiles had to come up to Israel's level to be saved, when actually the Jews had to go down to the level of the Gentiles to be saved. Instead of permitting their religious privileges (see vv. 1–5) to lead them to Christ, they used these privileges as a substitute for Christ.

No one will deny that there are many mysteries connected with divine sovereignty and human responsibility. Nowhere does God ask us to choose between these two truths, because they both come from God and are part of God's plan. They do not compete; they cooperate. The fact that we cannot fully understand *how* they work together does not deny the fact that they do. When a man asked Charles Spurgeon how he reconciled divine sovereignty and human responsibility, Spurgeon replied: "I never try to reconcile friends."

Applying God's Truth:

1. In what ways have you recently observed the evidence of God's divine sovereignty?

2. In what areas have you exercised your human responsibility?

3. If you had a friend pursuing "law righteousness," what advice would you offer to help that individual experience the freedom of "grace righteousness"?

Day 21

Willful Ignorance

Read Romans 10:1–13

> *"Since they did not know the righteousness that comes from God and sought to establish their own, they did not submit to God's righteousness."*
>
> ROMANS 10:3

Israel was ignorant of God's righteousness, not because they had never been told, but because they refused to learn. There is an ignorance that comes from lack of opportunity; but in their case, it was an ignorance that stemmed from willful, stubborn resistance to the truth. They were proud of their own good works and religious self-righteousness.

The godly Presbyterian preacher Robert Murray McCheyne was passing out tracts one day and handed one to a well-dressed lady. She gave him a haughty look and said, "Sir, you must not know who I am!"

In his kind way, McCheyne replied, "Madam, there is coming a day of judgment, and on that day it will not make any difference who you are!"

Everything about the Jewish religion pointed to the coming Messiah—their sacrifices, priesthood, temple services, religious festivals, and covenants. Their law told them they were sinners in need of a Savior. But instead of letting the law bring them to Christ (see Gal. 3:24), they worshiped their law and rejected their Savior. The law cannot give righteousness; it only leads sinners to the Savior who can give righteousness.

Applying God's Truth:

1. Do you think most ignorance about God is due to lack of opportunity to hear about Him, or rather is it resistance to the truth?

2. In what ways do your church sacraments and traditions point to Christ?

3. Can you think of people who seem to be so absorbed with tradition and ceremony that they miss the reality of a personal relationship with Jesus?

Day 22

Beautiful Feet

Read Romans 10:14–21

> *"How beautiful are the feet of those who bring good news!"*
> ROMANS 10:15

We must never minimize the missionary outreach of the church. While this passage relates primarily to Israel, it applies to all lost souls around the world. They cannot be saved unless they call upon the Lord Jesus Christ. But they cannot call unless they believe. Faith comes by hearing (see v. 17), so they must hear the message. How will they hear? A messenger must go to them with the message. But this means that God must call the messenger, and the messenger must be sent (see vv. 14–15). What a privilege it is to be one of His messengers and have beautiful feet!

As I was writing this chapter my phone rang, and one of the businessmen in our church reported another soul led to Christ. My caller had had serious spiritual problems a few years earlier, and I was able to help him. Since that time, he had led many to Christ, including some in his office. His phone call was to give me the good news that one of his associates had led a friend to Christ, another miracle in a spiritual chain reaction that had been going on for several years.

Some of us share the news here at home, but others are sent to distant places. In spite of some closed doors, there are still more open doors for the gospel than ever before; and we have better tools to work with.

Applying God's Truth:

1. Who is your ideal model for what an evangelist should be? What characteristics of the person do you admire?

2. Who are some people you could reach with the gospel who might not hear it from anyone else?

3. On a scale of 1 (least) to 10 (most), to what extent do you feel your church is committed to evangelistic outreach?

Day 23

Hard Truth

Read Romans 11:1–15

> *"What Israel sought so earnestly it did not obtain,*
> *but the elect did. The others were hardened."*
>
> ROMANS 11:7

For centuries people have been puzzled by the nation of Israel. The Roman government recognized the Jewish religion, but it still called the nation *secta nefaria*—a "nefarious sect." The great historian Arnold Toynbee classified Israel as "a fossil civilization" and did not know what to do with it. For some reason, the nation did not fit into his historical theories.

Paul devoted all of Romans 11 to presenting proof that God is not through with Israel. Israel is God's elect nation; He foreknew them, or chose them, and they are His. The fact that most of the nation has rejected Christ is no proof that God has finished with His people. In his day, Elijah thought that the nation had totally departed from God. He thought he was the only faithful Jew left, but he discovered that there were seven thousand more (see 1 Kings 19:13–18).

Paul referred to this "remnant" in Romans 9:27. At no time has the entire nation of Israel been true to the Lord. If a remnant had been saved, thus proving that God was not through with His people, then what had happened to the rest of the nation? They had been *hardened*. But Paul made it clear that the hardening of Israel is neither total nor final, and this fact is proof that God has a future for the nation.

Applying God's Truth:

1. Do you think any nation has ever surpassed Israel as God's "elect" nation?

2. What can you learn from the example set by the "remnant" of Israel?

3. In what ways do supposedly godly people become "hardened" in today's society?

Day 24

God's Remarkable Plans

Read Romans 11:16–36

"Just as you who were at one time disobedient to God have now received mercy as a result of their disobedience, so they too have now become disobedient in order that they too may now receive mercy as a result of God's mercy to you."

ROMANS 11:30–31

We must remember that God chose the Jews so that the Gentiles might be saved. "All peoples on earth will be blessed through you" was God's promise to Abraham (see Gen. 12:3). The tragedy was that Israel became exclusive and failed to share the truth with the Gentiles. They thought that the Gentiles had to become Jews in order to be saved. But God declared both Jews and Gentiles to be lost and condemned. This action meant that He could have mercy on all because of the sacrifice of Christ on the cross (see Rom. 11:28–32).

Having contemplated God's great plan of salvation for Jews and Gentiles, all Paul could do was sing a hymn of praise. As someone has remarked, "Theology becomes doxology!" Only a God as wise as our God could take the fall of Israel and turn it into salvation for the world! His plans will not be aborted, nor will His purposes lack fulfillment (see Isa. 46:10). No human being can fully know the mind of the Lord (see 1 Cor. 2:16); and the more we study His ways, the more we offer Him praise. Are we to conclude that God does *not* know what He is doing, and that the nation of Israel completely ruined His plans? Of course not! God is too wise to make plans that will not be fulfilled. Israel did not allow Him to rule, so He overruled!

Applying God's Truth:

1. Israel "became exclusive" with God's truth. Do you ever tend to be exclusive with whom you discuss the gospel?

2. Since God could turn the fall of Israel into the salvation of the world, can you think of one of your own "falls" that perhaps God will convert into good for a lot of people?

3. Has God ever "overruled" any of your plans? How did you feel when it happened?

Day 25

Full Surrender

Read Romans 12:1–6

> *"Offer your bodies as living sacrifices.... Do not conform any longer to the pattern of this world, but be transformed by the renewing of your mind. Then you will be able to test and approve what God's will is."*
>
> ROMANS 12:1–2

The mind controls the body, and the will controls the mind. Many people think they can control themselves and their lives by sheer "willpower," but usually they fail. (This was Paul's experience as recorded in 7:15–25.) It is only when we yield the will to God that His power can take over and give us the willpower (and the won't power!) that we need to be victorious Christians.

We surrender our will to God through disciplined prayer. As we spend time in prayer, we surrender our will to God and pray, with the Lord Jesus, "Not my will, but yours be done" (Luke 22:42). We must pray about everything, and let God have His way in everything.

For many years I have tried to begin each day by surrendering my body to the Lord. Then I spend time with His Word and let Him transform my mind and prepare my thinking for that new day. Then I pray and yield the plans of the day to Him and let Him work as He sees best. I especially pray about those tasks that upset or worry me—and He always sees me through. To have a right relationship with God, we must start the day by yielding to Him our bodies, minds, and wills.

Applying God's Truth:

1. What improvements would you like to make in your mind? Your will? Your body?

2. In what ways do you surrender each of these three areas to God? How could you be more completely surrendered in each case?

3. Can you think of specific ways that God has recently used your body, mind, and/or will to bring peace to your life and glory to Himself?

Day 26

Responding to Evil

Read Romans 12:17–13:14

"Do not be overcome by evil, but overcome evil with good."
ROMANS 12:21

As Christians we must not play God and try to avenge ourselves. Returning evil for evil, or good for good, is the way most people live. But we Christians must live on a higher level and return good for evil. Of course, this response requires *love*, because our first inclination is to fight back. It also requires *faith*, believing that God can work and accomplish His will in our lives and the lives of those who hurt us.

A friend of mine once heard a preacher criticize him over the radio and tell things that were not only unkind, but also untrue. My friend became very angry and was planning to fight back, when a godly preacher said, "Don't do it. If you defend yourself, then the Lord can't defend you. Leave it in His hands." My friend followed that wise counsel, and the Lord vindicated him.

As children of God, we must live on the highest level—returning good for evil. Anyone can return good for good and evil for evil. The only way to overcome evil is with good. If we return evil for evil, we only add fuel to the fire. But if we return good for evil, even if our enemy is not converted, we still experience the love of God in our own hearts and grow in grace (see 2 Peter 3:18).

Applying God's Truth:

1. When faced with evil, why are love and faith required to combat it?

2. Can you think of a personal example where you left an unjust situation in God's hands and allowed Him to defend you?

3. Is it possible to grow stronger and more mature even though you "lose" in conflicts with evil? If so, why do you think it is so rare to see people return good for evil?

Day 27

Jesus Is Lord of Other People Too

Read Romans 14:1–12

> *"Who are you to judge someone else's servant? To his own master he stands or falls. And he will stand, for the Lord is able to make him stand."*
>
> ROMANS 14:4

Paul explained to his readers that they did not have to give an account for anyone else but themselves. So they were to make sure that their account would be a good one. He was stressing the principle of lordship—make Jesus Christ the Lord of your life, and let Him be the Lord in the lives of other Christians as well.

Two of the most famous Christians in the Victorian era in England were Charles Spurgeon and Joseph Parker, both of them mighty preachers of the gospel. Early in their ministries they fellowshipped and even exchanged pulpits. Then they had a disagreement, and the reports even got into the newspapers. Spurgeon accused Parker of being unspiritual because he attended the theater. Interestingly enough, Spurgeon smoked cigars, a practice many believers would condemn. Who was right? Who was wrong? Perhaps *both* of them were wrong!

When it comes to questionable matters in the Christian life, cannot dedicated believers disagree without being disagreeable? "I have learned that God blesses people I disagree with!" a friend of mine told me one day, and I have learned the same thing. When Jesus Christ is

Lord in our lives, we permit Him to deal with His own servants as He wishes.

Applying God's Truth:

1. Do you think it's more difficult to allow Jesus to be Lord of your life, or of other peoples' lives? Why?

2. What activities do you think cause most disagreements among various groups of Christians? Why?

3. As the secular world views the Christian world, do you think they are more critical of our participation in the things we argue about, or the internal conflicts that arise about such participation? Explain.

Day 28

Preventing Stumbling; Encouraging Growth

Read Romans 14:13–23

"Let us stop passing judgment on one another. Instead, make up your mind not to put any stumbling block or obstacle in your brother's way."

Romans 14:13

When a child comes into a home, everything has to change. Mother and father are careful not to leave the scissors on the chair or anything dangerous within reach. But as the child matures, it is possible for the parents to adjust the rules of the house and deal with the youngster in a more adult fashion. It is natural for a child to stumble when learning to walk. But if an adult constantly stumbles, obviously something is wrong.

Young Christians need the kind of fellowship that will protect them and encourage them to grow. But they cannot be treated like "babies" all their lives! The older Christians must exercise love and patience and be careful not to cause them to stumble. But the younger Christians must "grow in the grace and knowledge of our Lord and Savior Jesus Christ" (2 Peter 3:18). As they mature in the faith, they can help other believers to grow. To gear the ministry of a Sunday school class or local church only to the "baby Christians" is to hinder their growth as well as the ministry of the more mature saints. The weak must learn from the strong, and the strong must love the weak. The result will be peace and maturity to the glory of God.

❧

Applying God's Truth:

1. Who are some Christians you feel are still "weak" in certain areas? Are you giving them time to mature? What are you doing to help them?

2. Would you say your Sunday school class, church service, Bible study group, and so forth are geared for "baby Christians," mature Christians, or those in between?

3. If you find that you are more (or less) mature than the others in most of the programs that are currently available to you, what do you think you should do?

Day 29

Time to Move On

Read Romans 15

"It has always been my ambition to preach the gospel where Christ was not known, so that I would not be building on someone else's foundation."

ROMANS 15:20

The vast area of opportunity in other parts of the empire kept Paul from visiting Rome sooner. He was not hindered from going to Rome by satanic opposition or physical obstacles, but by the challenge of completing his work right where he was. He was so faithful in his evangelistic outreach that he was able to say that he had no more place to minister in those parts (see v. 23). This statement did not mean that Paul had personally witnessed to every person in that area, but that he had taken the gospel throughout the region and had left behind witnessing churches and Christians who would carry on the work. Paul finished one job before he started another one, a good example for our evangelistic ministry today.

Paul's desire for many years had been to visit Rome and then move on to Spain (see v. 24), but there is no record that he ever did so. Tradition says that he did go to Spain, and to Britain, after he was released from prison, but church tradition is not always to be trusted.

Applying God's Truth:

1. If Paul came to your country to spread the gospel, where do you think he would start? Why?

2. How do you determine when it is time to "move on" from one Christian group (or project) to another?

3. Do you have any long-term spiritual goals or dreams? ("Someday I hope to …")

Day 30

Signing Off

Read Romans 16

"Now to him who is able to establish you by my gospel ...
so that all nations might believe and obey him—to the only wise
God be glory forever through Jesus Christ! Amen."

ROMANS 16:25–27

The closing benediction (see vv. 25–27) is the longest one Paul ever wrote. It reflects his special ministry to the Gentiles. The "mystery hidden for long ages past" that Paul writes about in verse 25 has to do with God's program of uniting believing Jews and Gentiles in the one body, the church (see Eph. 3). This was Paul's special message. It was because of this message that the Judaizers persecuted Paul, because they wanted to maintain Jewish privileges. Both Jews and Gentiles in the Roman churches needed to know what God's program was. Some of this program Paul had explained in chapters 9 through 11.

Christians are established by the truth, which explains why Paul wrote this letter: to explain God's plan of salvation to Christians so they would be established, and so they would share the truth with the lost. After all, we cannot really share with others something we do not have ourselves.

This means that our own study of Romans should make us more stable in the faith and more excited to share Christ with others. And the result: "to the only wise God be glory forever through Jesus Christ!"

Applying God's Truth:

1. If you wanted to encourage your church with a benediction of what God is able to do, what would you say to them?

2. If you had been a Gentile in the predominantly Jewish church at this time, how do you think you would have felt after reading Paul's letter to the Romans? Why?

3. If one theme of Romans is "Be right," in what ways do you feel you can be more right now than when you began reading through it?

Joy

The world talks about happiness, but God talks about joy. There is a difference, and when you learn what that difference is, your life will be different.

Happiness depends on happenings, what goes on around you. When your plans work out right, when you feel good, when problems are at a minimum, then you're happy. But when you wake up with a headache or the boss rearranges your schedule or somebody you love is hurting, then that happiness fades, and you're left feeling discouraged and defeated. You feel like quitting.

But life doesn't have to be that way. You can substitute joy for happiness and experience a whole new kind of life.

Joy doesn't depend on what goes on *around* you. It depends on what goes on *within* you. It is the result of a right relationship with God, a right attitude toward life, and a right faith in the power of Christ.

Happiness says, "I am the captain of my fate!" and courts disaster.

Joy says, "I can do everything through him who gives me strength" (Phil. 4:13) and marches to victory.

Paul didn't write the epistle to the Philippians from a comfortable library or an ivory tower. When he wrote it, he was a prisoner in Rome and *in danger of being executed any day.* Yet this letter is saturated with joy and rejoicing. Why? Because Paul was a man who knew Christ; he was a single-minded man with a mission to fulfill and a God to serve.

*Out*look helps to determine *out*come, and in this letter, Paul tells you how to have the kind of outlook that produces joy. He shares the "open secret" of having joy in spite of circumstances, people, things, or situations. He explains the basic principles of

Christian experience that can turn your life into a daily celebration of the joy of the Lord.

Yes, you will still have problems and battles and burdens, but you will find yourself overcoming instead of being overcome.

You will find yourself joyfully saying with Paul, "I can do everything through him who gives me strength."

Day 1

The Secret of Joy

Read Philippians 1:1–5

> *"I thank my God every time I remember you. In all my prayers*
> *for all of you, I always pray with joy because of your partnership*
> *in the gospel from the first day until now."*
>
> PHILIPPIANS 1:3–5

Paul's letter to the Philippian church is something of a missionary thank-you letter, but it is much more than that. It is the sharing of Paul's secret of Christian joy. At least nineteen times in these four chapters, Paul mentions joy, rejoicing, or gladness!

The unusual thing about the letter is this: Paul's situation was such that there appeared to be no reason for him to be rejoicing. He was a Roman prisoner, and his case was coming up shortly. He might be acquitted, or he might be beheaded! And, unfortunately, the believers at Rome (where he was being held) were divided—some were for him and some were against him. In fact, some of the Christians even wanted to make things more difficult for the apostle!

Yet, in spite of his danger and discomfort, Paul overflowed with joy. The secret of Christian joy is found in the way we believers think—our attitudes. After all, outlook determines outcome. As we think, so we are (see Prov. 23:7 KJV).

Philippians, then, is a Christian psychology book, based solidly on biblical doctrine. It is a book that explains the mind we must have if we are going to experience Christian joy in a world filled with trouble.

Applying God's Truth:

1. Can you recall a time or times when you experienced joy even under threatening or adverse situations?

2. What are some current situations that tend to keep you from experiencing joy? How can you keep from letting such situations rob you of joy?

3. As you go through these devotional readings, what are some things you hope to accomplish?

Day 2

Reducing Friction

Read Philippians 1:6–7

> *"Being confident of this, that he who began a good work in you will carry it on to completion until the day of Christ Jesus."*
>
> PHILIPPIANS 1:6

Isn't it remarkable that Paul was thinking of others and not of himself? As he awaited his trial in Rome, Paul's mind went back to the believers in Philippi, and every recollection brought him joy (see vv. 3–4). Read Acts 16; you may discover that some things had happened to Paul at Philippi, the memory of which could have produced sorrow. He had been illegally arrested and beaten, placed in stocks, and humiliated before the people. But even those memories brought joy to Paul. It was a source of joy to Paul to know that God was still working in the lives of his fellow believers in Philippi. The basis for joyful Christian fellowship is to have God at work in our lives day by day.

"There seems to be friction in our home," a concerned wife said to a marriage counselor. "I really don't know what the trouble is."

"Friction is caused by one of two things," said the counselor, and to illustrate he picked up two blocks of wood from his desk. "If one block is moving, and one is standing still, there's friction. Or, if both are moving but in opposite directions, there's friction. Now, which is it?"

"I'll have to admit that I've been going backward in my Christian life, and Joe has really been growing," the wife admitted. "What I need is to get back into fellowship with the Lord."

Applying God's Truth:

1. Does your spiritual growth seem to be an occasional thing, or do you see it as an ongoing process with God in control? Explain.

2. What are some things that cause friction in your spiritual development?

3. When did God begin a good work in you? How has your life changed since that time? What additional changes do you anticipate?

Day 3

Mark of Maturity

Read Philippians 1:8–10

> *"This is my prayer: that your love may abound more and more in knowledge and depth of insight, so that you may be able to discern what is best and may be pure and blameless until the day of Christ."*
>
> PHILIPPIANS 1:9–10

Paul found joy in his memories of the friends at Philippi and in his growing love for them. He also found joy in remembering them before the throne of grace in prayer. This is a prayer for maturity, and Paul began it with *love*. After all, if our Christian love is what it ought to be, everything else should follow. He prayed that they might experience *abounding* love and discerning love. Christian love is not blind! The heart and mind work together so that we have *discerning* love and loving discernment.

Paul wanted his friends to grow in discernment. The ability to distinguish is a mark of maturity. When a baby learns to speak, it may call every four-legged animal a "bow-wow." But then the child discovers that there are cats, dogs, white mice, cows, and other four-legged creatures. To a little child, one automobile is just like another, but not to a car-crazy teenager. Teens can spot the differences between models faster than their parents can even name the cars!

One of the sure marks of maturity is discerning love and loving discernment.

Applying God's Truth:

1. Think of ten close friends. How frequently do you pray for each one of them?

2. What do you think it means to have "discerning love" and "loving discernment"? In what ways is your love for others a discerning kind of love?

3. In your life do you seek what is good, or do you try to discern what is truly best?

Day 4

Fruitfulness versus Busyness

Read Philippians 1:11

> *"[I pray that you will be] filled with the fruit of righteousness that*
> *comes through Jesus Christ—to the glory and praise of God."*
>
> PHILIPPIANS 1:11

The difference between spiritual fruit and human religious activity is that fruit brings glory to Jesus Christ. Whenever we do anything in our own strength, we have a tendency to boast about it. True spiritual fruit is so beautiful and wonderful that no one can claim credit for it; the glory must go to God alone. This, then, is true Christian fellowship—a having-in-common that is much deeper than mere friendship.

Jerry was told that he had to go to New York City for special surgery, and he hated to go. "Why can't I have it done at home?" he asked his doctor. "I don't know a soul in that big, unfriendly city!" But when he and his wife arrived at the hospital, there was a pastor to meet them and invite them to stay at his home until they got settled. The operation was serious, and the wait in the hospital was long and difficult; but the fellowship of the pastor and his wife brought new joy to Jerry and his wife. They learned that circumstances need not rob us of joy if we will but permit those circumstances to strengthen the fellowship of the gospel.

Applying God's Truth:

1. What are some characteristics you would consider "the fruit of righteousness"?

2. In contrast, what are some of the things you would classify as only "religious activity"?

3. In which of your relationships would you say you experience genuine Christian fellowship? In which ones do you settle for "mere friendship"?

Day 5

Onward, Pioneers

Read Philippians 1:12–13

> *"It has become clear throughout the whole palace guard and to everyone else that I am in chains for Christ."*
>
> PHILIPPIANS 1:13

Everyone has heard of Charles Haddon Spurgeon, the famous British preacher, but few know the story of his wife, Susannah. Early in their married life, Mrs. Spurgeon became an invalid. It looked as though her only ministry would be encouraging her husband and praying for his work. But God gave her a burden to share her husband's books with pastors who were unable to purchase them. This burden soon led to the founding of the "Book Fund." As a work of faith, the "Book Fund" provided thousands of pastors with tools for their work. All this effort was supervised by Mrs. Spurgeon from her home. It was a pioneer ministry.

God still wants His children to take the gospel into new areas. He wants us to be pioneers, and sometimes He arranges circumstances so that we can be nothing else but pioneers. In fact, that is how the gospel originally came to Philippi! Paul had tried to enter other territory, but God had repeatedly shut the door (see Acts 16:6–10). Paul wanted to take the message eastward into Asia Minor, but God directed him to take it westward into Europe. What a difference it would have made in the history of mankind if Paul had been permitted to follow his plan!

Applying God's Truth:

1. Who are some people you know who aren't in prominent leadership roles, yet who have a lot of impact on others for advancing the gospel? What can you learn from such people?

2. What are some "new areas" where you might be able to carry the gospel?

3. Envision yourself as a spiritual "pioneer." What are some of the potential risks you need to be aware of? What are some of the potential benefits?

Day 6

Chains and Change

Read Philippians 1:14–17

*"Because of my chains, most of the brothers in the Lord have been encouraged
to speak the word of God more courageously and fearlessly."*

PHILIPPIANS 1:14

Sometimes God has to put "chains" on His people to get them to accomplish a "pioneer advance" that could never happen any other way. Young mothers may feel chained to the home as they care for their children, but God can use those "chains" to reach people with the message of salvation. Susannah Wesley was the mother of nineteen children, before the days of laborsaving devices and disposable diapers! Out of that large family came John and Charles Wesley, whose combined ministries shook the British Isles.

At six weeks of age, Fanny Crosby was blinded, but even as a youngster she determined not to be confined by the chains of darkness. In time, she became a mighty force for God through her hymns and gospel songs.

The secret is this: When we have the single mind (see Day 8), we look upon our circumstances as God-given opportunities for the furtherance of the gospel, and we rejoice at *what God is going to do* instead of complaining about *what God did not do*.

Applying God's Truth:

1. What are some ways in which you feel "chained"?

2. Do you have any regrets—or perhaps complaints—of times when you hoped God would work in a certain way, yet He didn't?

3. What are some ways you can overcome your chains and become a better witness for God?

Day 7

Larger Than Life

Read Philippians 1:18–20

> *"I eagerly expect and hope that I will in no way be ashamed,
> but will have sufficient courage so that now as always Christ will
> be exalted in my body, whether by life or by death."*
>
> PHILIPPIANS 1:20

Does Christ need to be magnified? After all, how can a mere human being ever magnify the Son of God? Well, the stars are much bigger than the telescope, and yet the telescope magnifies them and brings them closer to the viewer. The believer's body is to be a telescope that brings Jesus Christ closer to people. To the average person, Christ is a misty figure in history who lived centuries ago. But as the unsaved watch believers go through a crisis, they can see Jesus magnified and brought so much closer. To Christians with the single mind (see Day 8), Christ is with us here and now.

The telescope brings distant things closer, and the microscope makes tiny things look larger. To nonbelievers, Jesus is not very big. Other people and other things are far more important. But as they watch a Christian go through a crisis experience, they ought to be able to see how big Jesus Christ really is. The believer's body is a "lens" that makes a "little Christ" look very big, and brings a "distant Christ" very close.

Paul was not afraid of life or death! Either way, he wanted to magnify Christ in his body. No wonder he had joy!

Applying God's Truth:

1. Can you think of any recent ways in which you have magnified (exalted) God? If so, how?

2. Do you ever feel embarrassed when presenting the gospel to others? How do you muster "sufficient courage" to maintain an effective personal ministry?

3. What kind of "lens" do you provide through which friends and acquaintances see Christ? Do you magnify Him or tend to obscure the view in some way?

Day 8

The Single Mind

Read Philippians 1:21–24

"To me, to live is Christ and to die is gain."
PHILIPPIANS 1:21

James tells us that "a double-minded man [is] unstable in all he does" (James 1:8). Or, to use the old Latin proverb: "When the pilot does not know what port he is heading for, no wind is the right wind." The reason many Christians are upset by circumstances is because they do not cultivate "the single mind." Paul expressed this attitude of single-hearted devotion to Christ thus: "For to me, to live is Christ and to die is gain."

Paul discussed his difficult circumstances and faced them honestly. But his circumstances could not rob him of his joy because he was not living to enjoy circumstances; he was living to serve Jesus Christ. He was a man with purpose. He did not look at Christ through his circumstances; rather, he looked at his circumstances through Christ—and this viewpoint changed everything.

Paul rejoiced in his difficult circumstances because they helped to strengthen his fellowship with other Christians, gave him opportunity to lead others to Christ, and enabled him to defend the gospel before the courts of Rome. When we have the single mind, our circumstances work *for* us and not *against* us.

Applying God's Truth:

1. What do you think it means to be "single-minded," or to "have the single mind"?

2. What dominates your thoughts more than anything else?

3. Would you say your circumstances seem to influence your attitude about Jesus? Or does your relationship with Jesus tend to influence all your circumstances? Explain.

Day 9

People May Be Watching

Read Philippians 1:25–28

> *"Whatever happens, conduct yourselves in a manner*
> *worthy of the gospel of Christ."*
> PHILIPPIANS 1:27

My wife and I were visiting in London, and one day we decided to go to the zoo. We boarded the bus and sat back to enjoy the ride, but it was impossible to enjoy it because of the loud, coarse conversation of the passengers at the front of the bus. Unfortunately, they were Americans, and we could see the British around us raising their eyebrows and shaking their heads, as though to say, "Oh, yes, they're from America!" We were embarrassed because we knew that these people did not really represent the best of American citizens.

Paul is suggesting that we Christians are the citizens of heaven, and while we are on earth we ought to behave like heaven's citizens. He brings this concept up again in Philippians 3:20. It would be a very meaningful expression to the people in Philippi because Philippi was a Roman colony, and its citizens were actually Roman citizens, protected by Roman law. The church of Jesus Christ is a colony of heaven on earth! And we ought to behave like the citizens of heaven.

Applying God's Truth:

1. Why do you think Paul introduced his command with the phrase, "Whatever happens"?

2. Are you ever embarrassed by God? Are you ever embarrassed by other Christians? What's the difference?

3. How does your conduct relate to your expressions of faith? Try to think of some specific examples.

Day 10

Brothers in Arms

Read Philippians 1:29–30

> *"It has been granted to you on behalf of Christ not only
> to believe on him, but also to suffer for him."*
> PHILIPPIANS 1:29

Satan wants us to think that we are alone in the battle and that our difficulties are unique, but such is not the case. Paul reminded the Philippians that he was going through the same difficulties they were experiencing hundreds of miles from Rome! A change in geography is usually no solution to spiritual problems, because human nature is the same wherever we go, and the enemy is everywhere. Knowing that our fellow believers are also sharing in the battle should be an encouragement for us to keep going and to pray for them as we pray for ourselves.

Actually, going through spiritual conflict is one way we have to *grow in Christ.* God gives us the strength we need to stand firm against the enemy, and this confidence is proof to him that he will lose and that we are on the winning side. As we face the enemy and depend on the Lord, He gives us all that we need for battle. When the enemy sees our God-given confidence, it makes him fear.

So, having the single mind enables us to experience joy in the midst of battle because it produces in us consistency, cooperation, and confidence. We experience the joy of "spiritual teamwork" as we strive together for the faith of the gospel.

Applying God's Truth:

1. War buddies grow particularly close because of the sufferings they share. Can you think of some past trials that drew you close to other people?

2. How does it make you feel during times of stress to know that others have suffered—and continue to suffer—in similar ways?

3. How can being "single-minded" be an advantage during times of suffering?

Day 11

The Potential of Privileges

Read Philippians 2:1–6

"Your attitude should be the same as that of Christ Jesus: Who, being in very nature God, did not consider equality with God something to be grasped."

PHILIPPIANS 2:5–6

Certainly, as God, Jesus Christ did not need anything! He had all the glory and praise of heaven. With the Father and the Spirit, He reigned over the universe. But verse 6 states an amazing fact: He did not consider His equality with God as "something to be grasped." Jesus did not think of Himself; He thought of others. His outlook (or attitude) was that of unselfish concern for others. This is "the mind of Christ" (1 Cor. 2:16), an attitude that says, "I cannot keep my privileges for myself, I must use them for others; and to do this, I will gladly lay them aside and pay whatever price is necessary."

A reporter was interviewing a successful job counselor who had placed hundreds of workers in their vocations quite happily. When asked the secret of his success, the man replied: "If you want to find out what a worker is really like, don't give him responsibilities—give him *privileges*. Most people can handle responsibilities if you pay them enough, but it takes a real leader to handle privileges. A leader will use his privileges to help others and build the organization; a lesser man will use privileges to promote himself." Jesus used His heavenly privileges for the sake of others—for *our* sake.

Applying God's Truth:

1. Do you ever wish for fame and recognition? What are some of your specific desires? What do you think motivates such dreams?

2. When you have worked hard to earn certain privileges, how hard do you try to hold on to them? Can you think of recent instances when you willingly gave up your hard-earned privileges to help out someone else?

3. What does it mean to you that Jesus "did not consider equality with God something to be grasped"?

Day 12

Choosing Servanthood

Read Philippians 2:7–8

"But [Jesus] made himself nothing, taking the very nature of a servant, being made in human likeness. And being found in appearance as a man, he humbled himself and became obedient to death—even death on a cross!"

PHILIPPIANS 2:7–8

Thinking of "others" in an abstract sense only is insufficient; we must get down to the nitty-gritty of true service. Jesus thought of others and *became a servant!* When Christ was born at Bethlehem, He entered into a *permanent* union with humanity from which there could be no escape. He willingly humbled Himself so that He might lift us up! Jesus did not pretend to be a servant; He was not an actor playing a role. *He actually was a servant!* This was the true expression of His innermost nature. He was the God-Man, deity and humanity united in one, and He came as a servant.

Have you noticed as you read the four gospels that it was Jesus who served others, not others who served Jesus? He was at the beck and call of all kinds of people—fishermen, harlots, tax collectors, the sick, the sorrowing. In the Upper Room, when His disciples apparently refused to minister, Jesus arose, laid aside His outer garments, put on the long linen towel, and *washed their feet!* (See John 13:1–17.) He took the place of a menial slave! This was the submissive mind in action—and no wonder Jesus experienced such joy!

Applying God's Truth:

1. Think of your acts of service to others. What percentage of them would you say are absolutely genuine? What percentage might be considered "acting" or obligation?

2. What do you think was Jesus' secret to being such a good servant?

3. Do you believe there is a direct connection between serving others and receiving personal joy? Do your actions reflect your knowledge of this connection?

Day 13

A Submissive Mind

Read Philippians 2:9–11

"Therefore God exalted him ... that at the name of Jesus every knee should bow ... and every tongue confess that Jesus Christ is Lord, to the glory of God the Father."
PHILIPPIANS 2:9–11

Our Lord's exaltation began with His resurrection. When men buried the body of Jesus, that was the last thing any human hand did to Him. From that point on, it was God who worked. Men had done their worst to the Savior, but God exalted Him and honored Him. Men gave Him names of ridicule and slander, but the Father gave Him a glorious name!

People with the submissive mind, as they live for others, must expect sacrifice and service; but in the end, it is going to lead to glory. Joseph suffered and served for thirteen years, but then God exalted him and made him the second ruler of Egypt. David was anointed king when he was but a youth. He experienced years of hardship and suffering, but at the right time, God exalted him as king of Israel.

The joy of the submissive mind comes not only from helping others, and sharing in the fellowship of Christ's sufferings (see 3:10 KJV), but primarily from the knowledge that we are glorifying God. We are letting our light shine through our good works, and this action glorifies the Father in heaven. We may not see the glory today, but we will see it when Jesus comes and rewards His faithful servants.

Applying God's Truth:

1. On a scale of 1 (least) to 10 (most), how impatient do you feel when you serve others and don't receive an immediate reward or acknowledgment?

2. Is it enough for you to know that God will reward your good works eventually? Or is it still hard to keep doing good for people who don't seem to appreciate it?

3. How can you stay focused on God's promised rewards and not become disappointed when your good deeds go unrecognized?

Day 14

A Spiritual "Workout"

Read Philippians 2:12–13

"Continue to work out your salvation with fear and trembling, for it is God who works in you to will and to act according to his good purpose."

PHILIPPIANS 2:12–13

"Work out your salvation" does not suggest "work for your *own* salvation." To begin with, Paul was writing to people who were already "saints" (see 1:1), which means they had trusted Christ and had been set apart for Him. The Greek verb translated "work out" here carries the meaning of "work to full completion," such as working out a problem in mathematics. In Paul's day it was also used for working a mine; that is, getting out of the mine all the valuable ore possible or working a field so as to get the greatest harvest possible from it. The purpose God wants us to achieve is Christlikeness, "to be conformed to the likeness of his Son" (Rom. 8:29). There are problems in life, but God will help us to "work them out." Our lives have tremendous potential, like a mine or a field, and He wants to help us fulfill that potential.

The phrase "work out your salvation" probably had reference particularly to the special problems in the church at Philippi, but the statement also applies to individual Christians today. We are not to be "cheap imitations" of other people, especially "great Christians." We are to follow only what we see of Christ in their lives!

Applying God's Truth:

1. On a scale of 1 (least) to 10 (most), how hard would you say you try to "work out your salvation"?

2. Does your relationship with God still involve a degree of "fear and trembling," or have you begun to take some of your spiritual privileges for granted? Explain.

3. List some ways that God has worked in your life during the past few months, and thank Him for each one.

Day 15

Victory through Surrender

Read Philippians 2:14–18

"Even if I am being poured out like a drink offering on the sacrifice and service coming from your faith, I am glad and rejoice with all of you."

PHILIPPIANS 2:17

The world's philosophy is that joy comes from aggression: Fight everybody to get what you want, and you will get it and be happy. The example of Jesus is proof enough that the world's philosophy is wrong. He never used a sword or any other weapon; yet He won the greatest battle in history—the battle against sin and death and hell. He defeated hatred by manifesting love; He overcame lies with truth. Because He surrendered, He was victorious!

There is a twofold joy that comes to those who possess and practice the submissive mind: a joy hereafter and a joy here and now. In the day of Christ, God is going to reward those who have been faithful to Him. Faithful Christians will discover that their sufferings on earth have been transformed into glory in heaven! They will see that their work was not in vain. It was this same kind of promise of future joy that helped our Savior in His sufferings on the cross (see Heb. 12:1–2).

But we do not have to wait for the return of Christ to start experiencing the joy of the submissive mind. That joy is a present reality, and it comes through sacrifice and service.

Applying God's Truth:

1. Do you ever experience joy because of submission to others? In what specific ways?

2. What are some of the here-and-now joys you experience on a regular basis? How can you increase this level of joy?

3. What are some future joys you look forward to?

Day 16

In Search of Good Samaritans

Read Philippians 2:20–21

"I have no one else like [Timothy], who takes a genuine interest in your welfare. For everyone looks out for his own interests, not those of Jesus Christ."

PHILIPPIANS 2:20–21

A reporter in San Bernardino, California, arranged for a man to lie in the gutter on a busy street. Hundreds of people passed the man, but not one stopped to help him or even show sympathy!

Newspapers across the country a few years ago told how thirty-eight people watched a man stalk a young lady and finally attack her—and none of the spectators even picked up a phone to call the police!

A Kentucky doctor was driving down the highway to visit a patient when he saw an accident take place. He stopped and gave aid to the injured and then made his visit. One of the drivers he helped sued him!

Is it possible to be a "Good Samaritan" today? Must we harden our hearts in order to protect ourselves? Perhaps sacrifice and service are ancient virtues that somehow do not fit into our so-called modern civilization. It is worth noting that even in Paul's day, mutual concern was not a popular virtue. The Christians at Rome were not too interested in the problems at Philippi; Paul could not find *one person* among them willing to go to Philippi. Times have not changed too much.

Applying God's Truth:

1. Try to recall one time when you needed help but no one was willing to assist you in any way. How did you feel?

2. What are some of the positions in your church that are hardest to fill? Why do you think it is so tough to find volunteers for certain jobs?

3. What are some ways that people you know "look out for [their] own interests, not those of Jesus Christ"?

Day 17

A Servant's Reward

Read Philippians 2:22–30

> *"Timothy has proved himself, because as a son with his father he*
> *has served with me in the work of the gospel. I hope, therefore,*
> *to send him as soon as I see how things go with me."*
>
> PHILIPPIANS 2:22–23

Timothy knew the meaning of sacrifice and service, and God rewarded him for his faithfulness. To begin with, Timothy had the joy of helping others. To be sure, there were hardships and difficulties, but there were also victories and blessings. He had the joy of serving with the great apostle Paul and assisting him in some of his most difficult assignments.

But perhaps the greatest reward God gave to Timothy was to choose him to be Paul's replacement when the great apostle was called home. Paul himself wanted to go to Philippi, but he had to send Timothy in his place. But, what an honor! Timothy was not only Paul's "son," and Paul's servant, but he became Paul's substitute. His name is held in high regard by Christians today, something that young Timothy never dreamed of when he was busy serving Christ.

The submissive mind is not the product of an hour's sermon or a week's seminar or even a year's service. The submissive mind grows in us as, like Timothy, we yield to the Lord and seek to serve others.

Applying God's Truth:

1. Who is the person you know who best fits the description of Timothy given in this section?

2. Do you have anyone you can count on in the same way that Paul counted on Timothy? If not, how can you begin such a relationship with someone?

3. In the areas of your personal ministry, how are you training people to take your place when you move on to new places or other opportunities?

Day 18

No Confidence in the Flesh

Read Philippians 3:1–3

"It is we who are the circumcision, we who worship by the Spirit of God, who glory in Christ Jesus, and who put no confidence in the flesh."

PHILIPPIANS 3:3

The popular religious philosophy of today is "The Lord helps those who help themselves." It was also popular in Paul's day, and it is just as wrong today as it was then. By "the flesh," Paul means the old sinful nature that we received at birth. The Bible has nothing good to say about flesh, and yet most people today depend entirely on what they themselves can do to please God. Flesh only corrupts God's way on earth. It profits nothing as far as spiritual life is concerned (see John 6:63 KJV). It has nothing good in it (see Rom. 7:18 KJV). No wonder we should put no confidence in the flesh!

A lady was arguing with her pastor about this matter of faith and works. "I think that getting to heaven is like rowing a boat," she said. "One oar is faith, and the other is works. If you use both, you get there. If you use only one, you go around in circles."

"There is only one thing wrong with your illustration," replied the pastor. "Nobody is going to heaven *in a rowboat!*"

There is only one "good work" that takes sinners to heaven: the finished work of Christ on the cross.

Applying God's Truth:

1. What are some ways that you have observed people "put ... confidence in the flesh"?

2. Create your own model (pie chart, graph, etc.) to indicate how you think faith and works are related.

3. In contrast to putting confidence in the flesh, what does it mean to "worship by the Spirit of God"?

Day 19

Measuring Sticks

Read Philippians 3:4–7

> *"If anyone else thinks he has reasons to put confidence in the flesh,*
> *I have more.... But whatever was to my profit I now*
> *consider loss for the sake of Christ."*
>
> PHILIPPIANS 3:4, 7

Every Jew could boast of his own blood heritage. Some Jews could boast of their faithfulness to the Jewish religion. But Paul could boast of those things plus his zeal in persecuting the church (see vv. 5–6). We might ask, "How could a sincere man like Saul of Tarsus be so wrong?" The answer is simple: *He was using the wrong measuring stick!*

Like the rich young ruler (see Mark 10:17–22 KJV) and the Pharisee in Jesus' parable (see Luke 18:10–14), Saul of Tarsus was looking at the outside and not the inside. He was comparing himself with standards set by people, not by God. As far as obeying *outwardly* the demands of the law, Paul was a success, but he did not stop to consider the *inward* sins he was committing. In the Sermon on the Mount, Jesus made it clear that there are sinful *attitudes* and *appetites* as well as sinful *actions* (see Matt. 5:21–48).

When he looked at himself in comparison with others, Saul of Tarsus considered himself to be righteous. But one day he saw himself as compared with Jesus Christ! It was then that he changed his evaluations and values and abandoned "works righteousness" for the imputed righteousness of Jesus Christ (see Rom. 3:20–24).

Applying God's Truth:

1. Can you recall a time when you devoted a lot of time and energy to a project that didn't ultimately accomplish much? If so, how can you more effectively channel your efforts in the future?

2. Paul had worked very hard on his religion. Why do you think he was so quick to "consider [it] loss for the sake of Christ"?

3. Can you think of anything you may be clinging to that would be better to "consider loss" in order to continue to grow spiritually?

Day 20

Gaining and Losing

Read Philippians 3:8–11

> *"I consider everything a loss compared to the surpassing greatness of knowing Christ Jesus my Lord, for whose sake I have lost all things. I consider them rubbish, that I may gain Christ."*
>
> PHILIPPIANS 3:8

Remember Jim Elliot's words: "He is no fool who gives what he cannot keep to gain what he cannot lose." That is what Paul experienced. He lost his religion and his reputation, but he gained far more than he lost. In fact, the gains were so thrilling that Paul considered all other things nothing but garbage in comparison!

No wonder he had joy—his life did not depend on the temporal things of the world but on the eternal values found in Christ. Paul had the spiritual mind and looked at the things of earth from heaven's point of view. People who live for things are never really happy because they must constantly protect their treasures and worry lest they lose their value. Not so believers with the spiritual mind; their treasures in Christ can never be stolen, and they never lose their value (see Matt. 6:19–21).

Perhaps now is a good time for you to become an accountant and evaluate the things that matter most to you.

Applying God's Truth:

1. What is the single force that drives you more than any other?

2. What did you formerly value that you now consider "rubbish"? Why?

3. List the things you tend to value and contrast them with the eternal values made possible by Christ. In reviewing your list, do your feelings toward your possessions tend to change? If so, in what ways?

Day 21

Beyond Compare

Read Philippians 3:12–13

> *"I press on to take hold of that for which Christ Jesus took hold of me.
> Brothers, I do not consider myself yet to have taken hold of it."*
>
> PHILIPPIANS 3:12–13

Harry came out of the manager's office with a look on his face dismal enough to wilt the roses on the secretary's desk.

"You didn't get fired?" she asked.

"No, it's not that bad. But he sure did lay into me about my sales record. I can't figure it out; for the past month I've been bringing in plenty of orders. I thought he'd compliment me, but instead he told me to get with it." Later in the day, the secretary talked to her boss about Harry. The boss chuckled. "Harry is one of our best salesmen, and I'd hate to lose him. But he has a tendency to rest on his laurels and be satisfied with his performance. If I didn't get him mad at me once a month, he'd never produce!"

Many Christians are self-satisfied because they compare their "pressing on" with that of other Christians, usually those who are not making much progress. Had Paul compared himself with others, he would have been tempted to be proud and perhaps to let up a bit. After all, there were not too many believers in Paul's day who had experienced all that he had! But Paul did not compare himself with others; he compared himself *with himself* and *with Jesus Christ!* Mature Christians honestly evaluate themselves and strive to do better.

Applying God's Truth:

1. Do you think comparing yourself to others is always wrong? Why?

2. In a spiritual sense, can you identify any recent times when you may have tended to compare yourself to someone else rather than imitating the model Jesus has set?

3. When was the last time you tried objectively to evaluate your spiritual growth for the past month or year? How can you ensure that you don't "coast" too long without checking for progress?

Day 22

Finding a Specialty

Read Philippians 3:13–14

> *"But one thing I do: Forgetting what is behind and straining toward*
> *what is ahead, I press on toward the goal to win the prize for which*
> *God has called me heavenward in Christ Jesus."*
>
> PHILIPPIANS 3:13–14

Before the tragedy of the Chicago fire in 1871, D. L. Moody was involved in Sunday school promotion, YMCA work, evangelistic meetings, and many other activities; but after the fire, he determined to devote himself exclusively to evangelism. "One thing I do" became a reality to him. As a result, millions of people heard the gospel.

Believers must devote themselves to doing one thing well. No athlete succeeds by doing everything; he succeeds by *specializing*. There are those few athletes who seem proficient in many sports, but they are the exception. The winners are those who concentrate, who keep their eyes on the goal and let nothing distract them. They are devoted entirely to their calling. Like Nehemiah the wall-building governor, they reply to the distracting invitations, "I am carrying on a great project and cannot go down" (Neh. 6:3).

Concentration is the secret of power. If a river is allowed to overflow its banks, the area around it becomes a swamp. But if that river is dammed and controlled, it becomes a source of power. It is wholly a matter of values and priorities, focusing on the one thing that matters most.

Applying God's Truth:

1. In "straining toward what is ahead," would you say you are better in the short term or the long term?

2. What would you say is one area of ministry in which you could "specialize"?

3. Are you able to forget what is behind as you press on toward the goal to win the prize? Or are certain events of your past weighing you down and impeding your forward progress?

Day 23

Rules of the Game

Read Philippians 3:15–16

> *"All of us who are mature should take such a view of things.*
> *And if on some point you think differently, that too God will make*
> *clear to you. Only let us live up to what we have already attained."*
>
> PHILIPPIANS 3:15–16

It is not enough to press on toward the goal and win the prize; believers must also obey the rules. In the Greek games, the judges were very strict about this point. One day each of us Christians will stand before the judgment seat of Christ (see Rom. 14:10–12). The Greek word for "judgment seat" is *berna,* the very same word used to describe the place where the Olympic judges gave out the prizes! If we have disciplined ourselves to obey the rules, we will receive a prize.

Biblical history is filled with people who began their spiritual life with great success but failed at the end because they disregarded God's rules. They did not lose their salvation, but they did lose their rewards. It happened to Lot, Samson, Saul, and Ananias and Sapphira. And it can happen to us!

It is an exciting experience to run the race marked out for us daily, fixing our eyes on Jesus (see Heb. 12:1–2). It will be even more exciting when we experience that "high calling" (see Phil. 3:14 KJV), and Jesus returns to take us to heaven! Then we will stand before the *berna* to receive our rewards! It was this future prospect that motivated Paul, and it can also motivate us.

Applying God's Truth:

1. What "rules" of Christian living do you find hardest to obey on a regular basis?

2. How do you feel as you think about standing at the judgment seat of Christ to receive your rewards? Why?

3. What are three things you can do to ensure that you don't lose your rewards?

Day 24

Enemies of the Cross

Read Philippians 3:17–19

> *"As I have often told you before and now say again even with tears, many live as enemies of the cross of Christ."*
>
> PHILIPPIANS 3:18

The cross of Jesus Christ is the theme of the Bible, the heart of the gospel, and the chief source of praise in heaven. The cross is the proof of God's love for sinners and God's hatred for sin. In what sense were the Judaizers the "enemies of the cross of Christ"? For one thing, the cross ended the Old Testament religion. By His death and resurrection, Jesus accomplished a "spiritual circumcision" that made ritual circumcision unnecessary (see Col. 2:10–13). Everything the Judaizers advocated had been eliminated by the death of Christ on the cross.

Furthermore, everything that they lived for was condemned by the cross. Jesus had broken down the wall that stood between Jews and Gentiles (see Eph. 2:11–18), and the Judaizers were rebuilding that wall!

True believers crucify the flesh. They also crucify the world. Yet, the Judaizers were minding "earthly things" (see Phil. 3:19). It is the cross that is central in the life of believers. They do not glory in people, in religion, or in their own achievements; they glory in the cross (see Gal. 6:14).

Applying God's Truth:

1. Do you know people you would consider "enemies of the cross of Christ"? How would you describe them?

2. What are your feelings toward people who are openly hostile to Christian teaching? Why?

3. How much thought have you put into the significance of the cross? Would you say you "glory" in the cross, or do you need to think some more about this subject?

Day 25

Dual Citizenship

Read Philippians 3:20–21

> *"Our citizenship is in heaven. And we eagerly await*
> *a Savior from there, the Lord Jesus Christ."*
>
> PHILIPPIANS 3:20

The citizens of Philippi were privileged to be Roman citizens away from Rome. When babies were born in Philippi, it was important that their names be registered on the legal records. When lost sinners trust Christ and become citizens of heaven, their names are written in "the book of life" (see Phil. 4:3).

Citizenship is important. When we travel to another country, it is essential that we have a passport that proves our citizenship. None of us wants to suffer the fate of Philip Nolan in the classic tale *The Man Without a Country* written by Edward Everett. Because he cursed the name of his country, Nolan was sentenced to live aboard ship and never again see his native land or even hear its name or news about its progress. For fifty-six years he was on an endless journey from ship to ship and sea to sea, and finally he was buried at sea. He was truly a "man without a country."

As Christians our names are written in "the book of life," and this is what determines our final entrance into the heavenly country. When we confess Christ on earth, He confesses us in heaven (see Matt. 10:32 KJV). Our names are written down in heaven, and there they stand written forever.

Applying God's Truth:

1. Think of some groups and organizations to which you belong. What privileges do you have as a member of each group?

2. What privileges are you entitled to as a "citizen of heaven"?

3. What are your responsibilities as a "citizen of heaven"?

Day 26

The Antidote to Worry

Read Philippians 4:1–5

> *"Rejoice in the Lord always. I will say it again: Rejoice!*
> *Let your gentleness be evident to all. The Lord is near."*
>
> PHILIPPIANS 4:4–5

If anybody had an excuse for worrying, it was the apostle Paul. Two of his beloved Christian friends at Philippi were disagreeing with one another, and he was not there to help them. We have no idea what Euodia and Syntyche were disputing about, but whatever it was, it was bringing division into the church (see vv. 2–3). Along with the potential division at Philippi, Paul had to face division among the believers at Rome (see 1:14–17). Added to these burdens was the possibility of his own death! Yes, Paul had a good excuse to worry—but he did not! Instead, he took time to explain the secret of victory over worry.

The Old English root from which we get our word "worry" means "to strangle." Any of us who have ever really worried know how worry does strangle! In fact, worry has definite physical consequences: headaches, neck pains, ulcers, even back pains. Worry affects our thinking, our digestion, and even our coordination.

The antidote to worry is the secure mind: "The peace of God … will guard your hearts and your minds in Christ Jesus" (4:7). When we have the secure mind, the peace of God guards us and the God of peace guides us! With that kind of protection—why worry?

Applying God's Truth:

1. What are three things you are worried about right now? If you begin to rejoice about other, more positive things, how do you think your worries would be affected?

2. Do you think it is really possible to rejoice always? Explain.

3. How can you reduce your amount of worrying in the future?

Day 27

Mind Guarding

Read Philippians 4:6–7

> *"Do not be anxious about anything, but in everything, by prayer and petition, with thanksgiving, present your requests to God."*
>
> PHILIPPIANS 4:6

Paul counsels us to take everything to God in prayer. "Don't worry about *anything*, but pray about *everything!*" is his admonition. We are prone to pray about the "big things" in life and forget to pray about the "little things"—until they grow and become big things! Talking to God about *everything* that concerns us and Him is the first step toward victory over worry.

The result is that the "peace of God" (v. 7) guards our hearts and our minds. We remember that Paul was chained to a Roman soldier, guarded day and night. In like manner, "the peace of God" stands guard over the two areas that create worry—the heart (wrong feeling) and the mind (wrong thinking). When we give our hearts to Christ in salvation, we experience "peace *with* God" (Rom. 5:1); but the "peace *of* God" takes us a step further into His blessings. This does not mean the absence of trials on the outside, but it does mean a quiet confidence within, regardless of circumstances, people, or things.

Applying God's Truth:

1. What are some "little things" in your life that concern you, yet that you may feel are too insignificant to pray about? (Whatever you think of, commit it to prayer, and trust God to deal with the little things as well as the big ones.)

2. We tend to think of peace as an inner emotion. How do you feel when you envision God's peace as something that can protect you from outside influences?

3. What requests do you need to present to God today? What reasons do you have to offer thanksgiving today?

Day 28

The Right Balance

Read Philippians 4:8–9

*"Whatever is true, whatever is noble, whatever is right, whatever is pure,
whatever is lovely, whatever is admirable—if anything is excellent or
praiseworthy—think about such things. Whatever you have learned
or received or heard from me, or seen in me—put it into practice."*

PHILIPPIANS 4:8–9

Paul balanced four activities: "learned" and "received" and "heard" and "seen." It is one thing to *learn* a truth, but quite another to *receive* it inwardly and make it a part of our inner self. Facts in the head are not enough; we must also have truths in the heart. In Paul's ministry, he not only taught the Word but also lived it so that his listeners could see the truth in his life. Paul's experience ought to be our experience. We must learn the Word, receive it, hear it, and do it.

The peace of God is one test of whether or not we are in the will of God. If we are walking with the Lord, then the peace of God (see v. 7) and the God of peace (see v. 9) exercise their influence over our hearts. Whenever we disobey, we lose that peace, and we know we have done something wrong.

Right praying, right thinking, and right living—these are the conditions for having the secure mind and victory over worry.

Applying God's Truth:

1. Of learning, receiving, hearing, and seeing God's Word, which do you feel you do best? In which area do you need the most work?

2. What can you do to keep your thoughts true, pure, lovely, and so forth? How do you prevent less noble thoughts from sneaking in?

3. What are some things you can "think about" right now that will help purify your thought patterns?

Day 29

Learning Contentment

Read Philippians 4:10–12

> *"I have learned to be content whatever the circumstances. I know what it is to be in need, and I know what it is to have plenty."*
>
> PHILIPPIANS 4:11–12

Contentment is not complacency, nor is it a false peace based on ignorance.

Complacent believers are unconcerned about others, while contented Christians want to share their blessings. Contentment is not escape from the battle, but rather an abiding peace and confidence in the midst of the battle. Two words in verse 11 are vitally important— "learned" and "content."

The verb "learned" means "learned by experience." Paul's spiritual contentment was not something he had immediately after he was saved. He had to go through many difficult experiences of life in order to learn how to be content.

The word "content" actually means "contained." It is a description of those whose resources are within them so that they do not have to depend on substitutes without. The Greek word means "self-sufficient" and was a favorite word of the Stoic philosophers. But as Christians we are not sufficient in ourselves; we are sufficient in Christ. Because Christ lives within us, we are adequate for the demands of life (see v. 13).

Applying God's Truth:

1. What are your major sources of discontentment? What causes you to be content?

2. Do you think you can learn to be content most of the time without undergoing suffering first? Why?

3. What would have to happen before you feel that you could be content—no matter what happens?

Day 30

Needs and Greeds

Read Philippians 4:13–23

"I can do everything through him who gives me strength."
PHILIPPIANS 4:13

God has not promised to supply all our "greeds." When we are in the will of God, serving for the glory of God, then we will have every need met. Hudson Taylor often said, "When God's work is done in God's way for God's glory, it will not lack for God's supply."

A young pastor came to a church that had been accustomed to raising its annual budget by means of suppers, bazaars, and the like. He told his officers he could not agree with their program. "Let's pray and ask God to meet every need," he suggested. "At the end of the month, pay all the bills and leave my salary till the last. If there isn't enough money for my salary, then I'm the one who will suffer, and not the church. But I don't think anybody is going to suffer!" The officers were sure that both the pastor and the church would die, but such was not the case. Each month every bill was paid, and at the end of the year there was a surplus in the treasury for the first time in many years.

Contentment comes from adequate resources. Our resources are the providence of God, the power of God, and the promises of God. These resources made Paul sufficient for every demand of life, and they can make us sufficient too.

Applying God's Truth:

1. Are you careful to separate your needs from your "greeds"? Can you think of anything you have been praying for that may not be a legitimate need?

2. Can you think of anything you have been wanting to ask God for, yet are hesitant because it seems too great a request? Based on today's verse, are you ready now to ask for it?

3. Can you think of ways that God might use you to supply someone else's need?